City of Angels

In and Around LOS ANGELES

by Julie Jaskol & Brian Lewis

illustrated by ELISA KLEVEN

DUTTON CHILDREN'S BOOKS ▼ NEW YORK

To the memory of my mother, Lorraine Art Schneider,
who filled my L.A. childhood with art and love
E.K.

To the children of Los Angeles, especially Rose and Walker
J.J. & B.L.

Many thanks to our L.A. families who helped us so much: Stan and Sally Schneider, Carol Schneider, Susie Zallen, Sylvia Morales, Cathy Davies, Anita Jaskol, and Stan and Jann Jaskol. Thanks also to Donna, Sara, and Alissa.

We would also like to extend our thanks to: Afrikan Color Scheme; Jay Aldrich, Autry Museum of Western Heritage; Elayne Alexander, Venice Historical Society; Elena Allen; Armando, Mariachi Photo Studio; Linda Barth, L.A. City Department of Recreation and Parks; Jeffrey Baskin, Paramount Pictures; Brian Breyé, Museum in Black; California Lawyers for the Arts; Canter's Delicatessen; Canton Poultry; Capitol Records; Casa del Musico; CBS; Christine Chrisman, Los Angeles Dodgers; Darlene Daniels, Pages Books for Children; Du-par's Restaurant; Doug Dutton, Dutton's Books; Mike Eberts, *Griffith Park: A Centennial History;* Filomena Eriman, Grand Central Market; William Estrada, El Pueblo de Los Angeles Historical Monument; Greg Fischer; Pamela Fisher; Louise Gabriel, Santa Monica Historical Society; Marty Geimer, Beverly Hills Historical Society; Mark Greenfield, Watts Towers; Eugene Grigsby, UCLA; Chris Hills, Los Angeles County Natural History Museum; The Hollywood Bowl; Hong Ning Co.; Thacher Hurd; Jacquie Israel, Storyopolis; The Israel Levin Senior Center; Lucy Jones, U.S. Geological Survey; Sachiko Kimura, Little Tokyo Business Association; Chris M. Komai, Japanese American National Museum; Kongo Square; Tom LaBonge, Office of the Mayor; Dr. Lanier, Kids' Dental Kare; Michael Laxineta; Leimert Park Eyewear; Susan Malk, The White Rabbit Children's Bookstore; Christy McAvoy, Historic Resources Group; Gary McCarthy, *Los Angeles Independent;* Cindy McNaughton, Central Library; Mann's Chinese Theatre; Mariachi Appliance Store; John Michael, Plaza Commons, Inc., at California Plaza; Eugene W. Moy, Chinese Historical Society of Southern California; Danny Muñoz, Echo Park Historical Society; Musso & Frank Grill; NBC; Judy Nelson, Mrs. Nelson's Toy and Book Shop; Al Nodal, City of Los Angeles Cultural Affairs Department; Phil Orland, Angels Gate Park; José-Luis Orozco; The Page Museum at the La Brea Tar Pits; Jan Palchikoff, Santa Monica Pier Restoration Corporation; Mark Panatier, Farmers Market; Philippe French Dipped Sandwiches; Jean Bruce Poole, El Pueblo de Los Angeles Historical Monument; Mary Rainwater, The Los Angeles Free Clinic; Mr. Ramen; Catherine Rice, City of Los Angeles Cultural Affairs Department; The Honorable Mark Ridley-Thomas, Los Angeles City Councilman; Hitoshi Sameshima, Japanese American National Museum; Santa Cecilia Restaurant; Joy Sekimura; Ingeborg Sepp, Caltech; Avra Shapiro and Liebe Geft, Simon Wiesenthal Center Museum of Tolerance; Jody Shapiro, Adventures for Kids; Michael Stone, UCLA; Cooke Sunoo, Community Redevelopment Agency; Yasuyuki Suzuki, Miyako Inn & Spa; Betty Takeuchi, San Marino Toy and Book Shoppe; Mark Teichrow, *Los Angeles Times;* Alex Uhl, A Whale of a Tale; Earl Underwood, Leimert Park Fine Art Gallery; The Vision Theater; Msgr. Francis J. Weber, Archdiocese of Los Angeles Archival Center; Sydney Weisman & David Hamlin; John Welborne, Angels Flight Railway Foundation; Earl White, The Dance Collective; Gloria Williams, Norton Simon Museum; Larry Wilson, *Pasadena Star-News;* Wonder Bakery; Cy Wong, Chinese Historical Society of Southern California; Mike Woo; Cynthia Wornham, The J. Paul Getty Trust; and Liana Yamasaki, Tournament of Roses.

CIP Data is available.

Published in the United States 1999 by Dutton Children's Books, a division of Penguin Putnam Books for Young Readers
345 Hudson Street, New York, New York 10014   http://www.penguinputnam.com/yreaders/index.htm

Designed by Sara Reynolds and Richard Amari   Printed in Hong Kong   First Edition
1 2 3 4 5 6 7 8 9 10   ISBN 0-525-46214-7

CONTENTS

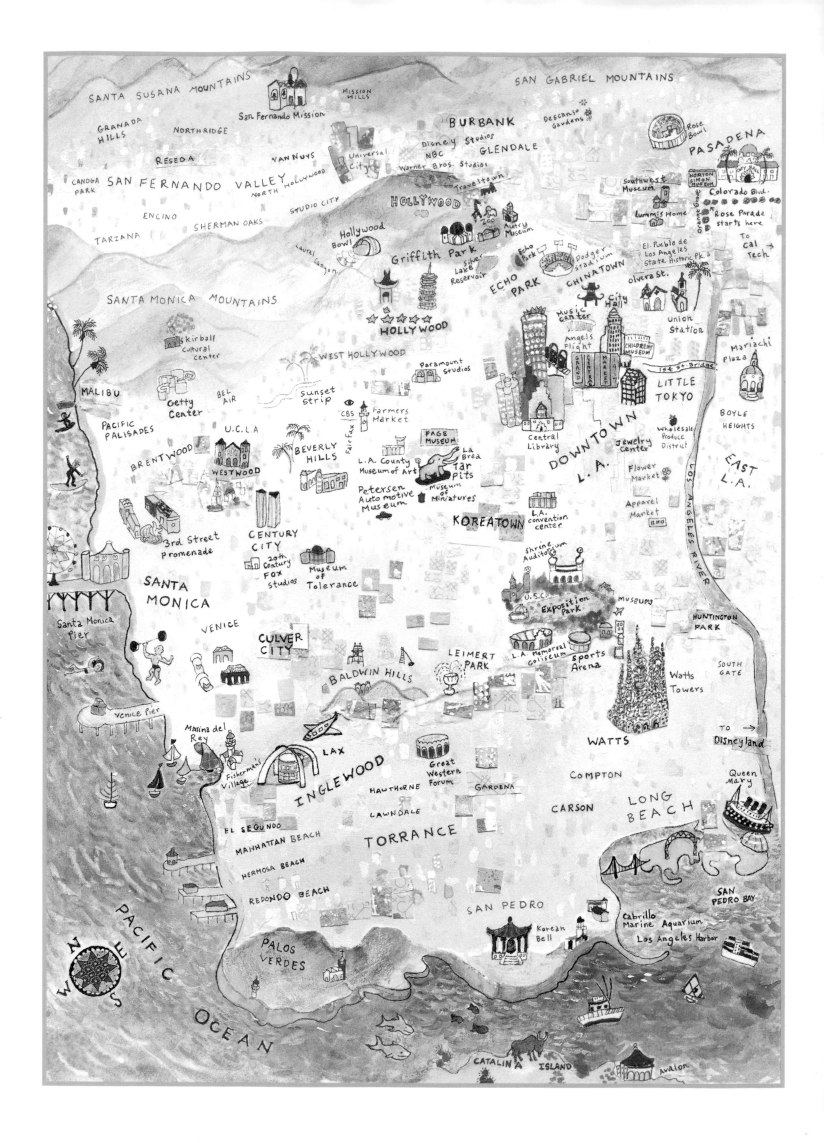

On a hot summer day in 1769, an expedition of Spanish soldiers and Franciscan friars set up camp by a river on a broad plain that would later come to be known as the Los Angeles basin. Having the day before celebrated the Feast of Our Lady Queen of the Angels, a Catholic holiday, they named their campsite "El Pueblo de la Reina de Los Angeles" ("The Town of the Queen of the Angels"). By 1850, when the campsite had grown into a small town and California had been admitted to the union, the name had shrunk to Los Angeles, Spanish for "the angels."

Isolated from the rest of the nation by mountain ranges to the north, east, and south and the vast Mojave Desert beyond them, Los Angeles lay near the Pacific Ocean, but had no natural harbor. It didn't even have a reliable water source. Not long after the Spanish explorers camped on its green banks, the river flooded and changed its course, running south to the sea in far-off San Pedro. The Los Angeles basin was left dry and dusty.

Yet a city grew because people determinedly remade the land. By the early 20th century, railroads linked Los Angeles to the rest of the nation; a port connected it to the rest of the world; and a pipeline from Owens Valley in the north supplied a steady flow of water. Los Angeles' balmy climate and the vast possibilities of its wide open spaces irresistibly pulled people from older, colder cities back east, and from other countries as well.

Expanding without the rigid grids of planned communities, Los Angeles sprawled this way and that, eventually stretching some 465 square miles, gobbling up smaller cities in its path. Pasadena, Beverly Hills, and Santa Monica managed to keep their independent city councils and city halls, but Hollywood, Venice, and other smaller towns became neighborhoods in L.A. Today nearly 4 million residents make it the second largest city in the U.S. The city of Los Angeles is contained within Los Angeles County, which covers more than 4,000 square miles, and consists of 88 separate cities and more than 9 million people. The region boasts the world's highest rate of immigration, particularly from Asia and Latin America.

Streets change their character from block to block in L.A. Teeming, densely packed neighborhoods can quickly give way to quiet, lush areas where huge homes hide behind tall hedges. Storefront signs in Armenian dissolve into signs in Korean or Thai. Mediterranean-style houses with red-tiled roofs are flanked by English country cottages and L.A.'s unique "dingbat" apartment buildings, little more than boxes on stilts.

Some people sum up the city in easy-to-grasp clichés: convertibles, palm trees, cell phones; or, alternatively, earthquakes, riots, and annual brush fires that threaten to wipe Los Angeles off its canyons and hillsides. Writers have long tried to distill Los Angeles. Humorist Dorothy Parker sniffed dismissively that "Los Angeles is 72 suburbs in search of a city." Historian Carey McWilliams said it was like "a ringside seat at the circus." Novelist Raymond Chandler declared, "Los Angeles was just a big dry sunny place with ugly homes and no style, but goodhearted and peaceful."

This book does not try to offer a comprehensive or complete view of Los Angeles. It presents a collection of neighborhoods and landmarks that offer some insight into the city's history, diversity, and range. Our apologies to you if we left out your favorite places. We left out many of our favorite places, too. The selections takes you through a year in Los Angeles, beginning with Chinese New Year in Chinatown. An angel or two is tucked away in each large picture for good measure.

Chinatown

The New Year roars into Chinatown each winter with the colorful Dragon Parade down Broadway. In the Chinese zodiac, the powerful dragon brings the four blessings of riches, harmony, virtue, and longevity.

The dragon has been dancing down these streets for more than 100 years, when Chinatown was a jumble of narrow dirt roads. Beginning in the mid-1800s, Chinese immigrants working in the gold mines and on railroads moved south and settled in the northeastern part of downtown. Others came from China to join them in a new life in a new land. They created a bustling neighborhood jam-packed with stores

and restaurants that reminded them of their homeland.

That first Chinatown fell to the bulldozer in the 1930s in order for the city to build a new railway terminal. With its heavy wooden beams and gilded ceilings, Union Station stands majestically, but it came at the cost of a lively community. In 1938, Chinatown rebuilt itself a few blocks to the northwest in a more open style suited to the times, with plazas and broad streets. Many of the original stores and restaurants survive, run by descendants of the first proprietors. Chinatown today serves as a center of Cambodian and Vietnamese commerce as well as Chinese.

Olvera Street

Every year on the day before Easter Sunday, Olvera Street and the old plaza go to the dogs—and cats, goats, pigs, and even lizards and snakes. For the Blessing of the Animals, hundreds of people visit this historic street near the site of the Spanish settlement of "El Pueblo de la Reina de Los Angeles," or "The Town of the Queen of the Angels." In 1780, the Spanish governor offered land, horses, plows, and tools, plus ten pesos a month, to any farmer who would settle the new *pueblo* as a colony of Spain. The following year, 11 families of mixed Spanish, African, and Indian heritage arrived. They built the *zanja madre*, or mother ditch, to bring water from the nearby Los Angeles River. Farms and ranches flourished, and Los Angeles grew. In 1926, a woman named Christine Sterling was shocked to see that Olvera Street had become a dirty alley, its buildings on the verge of collapse. She launched a campaign to save it, and on Easter Sunday in 1930, the street opened as a Mexican marketplace. The Blessing of the Animals began as part of her effort to reintroduce authentic Mexican culture. "We bless these animals for all they have done," a priest says, sprinkling holy water on each animal's head. "And for tendering a service to the human race."

Los Angeles Times Festival of Books at UCLA

There's no place book lovers would rather be each spring than the *Los Angeles Times* Festival of Books, where they can celebrate the joy of books and reading. They may even get a chance to talk with their favorite authors—or hug a beloved costumed character in the special children's area. Sponsored by the *Los Angeles Times*, the city's largest and most influential daily newspaper, the Festival of Books features booths jammed full of booksellers' and publishers' latest offerings. On various stages throughout the UCLA campus, authors read from their works and discuss them.

The stately campus of UCLA forms a majestic backdrop for the festivities. The regal red-brick buildings rose in the late 1920s as the centerpiece of a master plan that also included homes and businesses in the nearby community of Westwood. Although 100 years younger than most great universities, UCLA consistently ranks among the nation's top schools for graduate and undergraduate education. Its research libraries are among the largest in the country.

Today Westwood contains the highest concentration of single-screen movie theaters in the world, but during the *Los Angeles Times* Festival of Books, the written word takes center stage.

Little Tokyo

You walk through history as you walk along First Street in Little Tokyo. Imprinted on the sidewalk in various places are the words of generations of Japanese immigrants and the names and dates of the many businesses that have lined the street since 1885. By 1908, so many Japanese had settled in this downtown neighborhood that their American-born neighbors called it Little Tokyo.

Outside the Japanese American National Museum, a replica of an old box camera projects scenes of life from the Manzanar prison camp onto a window. The pictures remind viewers how World War II tragically interrupted the orderly flow of life on First Street. At war with Japan, the U.S. government ordered the imprisonment of all West Coast residents of Japanese ancestry. Images of suitcases stamped into the First Street sidewalk recall this painful, forced relocation. After three long years in prison, Japanese Americans returned to Little Tokyo in 1945 and reclaimed their community. Today noodle shops, Buddhist temples, and gardens form the backdrop for both daily life and special events. People come to Little Tokyo from all over to celebrate their customs and history. One such celebration is Children's Day, when carp flags fly to honor children around the world.

Griffith Park

The largest city park in the nation, Griffith Park sprawls across more than 4,000 acres of hillside—nearly six times as big as New York City's Central Park and four times larger than Golden Gate Park in San Francisco. From the top of the park's brush-covered mountains, hikers can see the entire Los Angeles basin stretching south. In the canyon below, visitors can cool off near a stream lined with lush green ferns. And in between are rolling lawns where families picnic and play in the big, shared backyard that is Griffith Park.

"Public parks are the safety valve of great cities," said Griffith J. Griffith, an eccentric millionaire who donated

the park to the people of Los Angeles in 1896. After looking through a telescope at nearby Mount Wilson, Griffith resolved to build an observatory at the park. "If all mankind could look through that telescope, it would revolutionize the world," he said.

With its three copper-covered domes and commanding presence overlooking the city, the Griffith Observatory quickly became one of Los Angeles's most recognizable monuments. Just as Griffith intended, gazing at the stars or hiking in the park can make you forget you're in the second-largest city in the United States.

Watts Towers

The lacy, delicate spires of the Watts Towers rise
dreamlike from the railroad tracks, chain-link fences,
and small bungalows of the surrounding South-Central
neighborhood. Nearly 10 stories high, the towers are the
work of one man: Simon Rodia. He toiled alone for more
than three decades, without scaffolding, welding torches, or
even a formal plan—only the graceful vision in his mind.

Every night after work and on the weekends, he built
fanciful structures made of steel rods and wrapped them in
wire mesh. Section by section, he covered the mesh with wet
cement and into it pressed colorful bits and pieces of things
he found. Climbing the towers like trees, Rodia adorned
them with pieces of green and blue bottles, seashells, tiles,
mirrors, and plates. He etched hearts, designs, and words
into the walls and floors. In his solitary, painstaking way he
also built a ship, a gazebo, birdbaths, walkways, fountains,
and a sculpted "cactus garden."

No one knows why Rodia began his labor of love, and no
one knows why he stopped. In 1955, he deeded the towers
to a neighbor (who as a child had brought him dishes and
bottles) and moved to Northern California. Shunning
attention, he lived alone and never saw his towers again.
Asked years later why he built the towers, Rodia said simply:
"I set out to do something big, and I did."

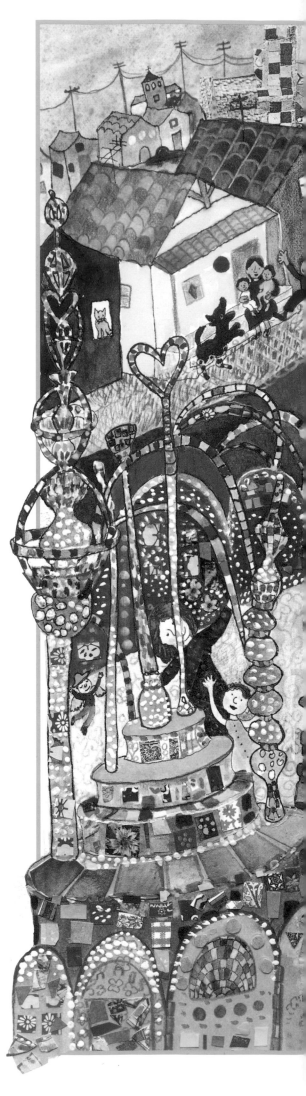

Exposition Park

The 16,000 rosebushes in the Exposition Park Rose Garden make this the most fragrant spot in town—and one of the most photographed. Along with the blossoms come dozens of photographers, taking pictures of families posing for keepsakes. When the park opened south of downtown in 1872, it was called Agricultural Park, and farmers displayed their harvests there. Horses, dogs, and even camels competed along a racetrack that lay where the rosebushes bloom today. As Los Angeles spread southward, the park area became more fashionable. The University of Southern California, built in 1880, attracted distinguished scholars.

Soon the city's most influential families moved into the neighborhood, and they didn't like the racing or the gambling that came with it. In 1913, a garden replaced the racetrack, and the park became a cultural center with grand museums.

The museums have changed with the times. Today a fighter jet pops out of the wall of the Aerospace Museum. The California African-American Museum chronicles the black experience in America. A priceless collection of stuffed mammals, reptiles, and birds lines the halls of the Museum of Natural History, and at the California Science Center you can explore the wonders of our world—and worlds beyond.

Page Museum at the La Brea Tar Pits

Where cars whiz by today on Wilshire Boulevard, mammoths and saber-toothed cats once roamed. Now all that remains of the Ice Age mammals that lived there as far back as 40,000 years ago can be found inside the Page Museum and deep within nearby pits of tar ("tar" is *brea* in Spanish).

Since the early 1900s, scientists have recovered millions of fossils, along with the 9,000-year-old skull and partial skeleton of a woman—the only human remains ever found in the pits. All these things were preserved in the sticky asphalt produced by a vast, subterranean sea of petroleum that oozed to the surface during warm weather year after year for 30,000 years. Rainwater collected on top of the tar, and when animals came to drink, they got stuck in the goo. They died from starvation—or were killed by predators—and their bones slowly sank into the muck. Today a landscaped tar pit in front of the museum features life-size statues of mammoths struggling to break free of the tar's grip, making vivid this long-ago drama.

During the warm months of summer, little black puddles of asphalt still dot the museum grounds, and scientists continue to dig fossils from excavations on the site, piecing together what life was like in Los Angeles all those centuries ago.

Santa Monica and Venice

For generations, Angelenos have made the neighboring coastal city of Santa Monica, just west of L.A., their playground. In the mid-1800s, people endured a daylong buggy ride from Los Angeles to camp on the wide, sandy beach and bathe in the ocean. By the turn of the 20th century, hundreds of thousands of passengers took the streetcar to the beach each year. They came to stroll along gigantic piers jutting into the oceans, and to enjoy the dance halls, indoor saltwater swimming pools, roller coasters, and funhouses along the beach. Today Santa Monica Pier, built in 1909, houses a new amusement park and an old merry-go-round

with hand-carved horses and the oldest organ in the United States, constructed in 1900.

In 1904, an ambitious entrepreneur named Abbot Kinney transformed salt marshes next to Santa Monica into a replica of Venice, Italy, complete with authentic Italian boat-men steering imported gondolas along a series of canals. Eager to have its own shoreline, the city of Los Angeles con-solidated with Venice in 1926 and, over the protests of some residents, paved most of the canals. Today the canals that remain have been restored, and ducks and boaters once again paddle along them.

Hollywood

Hollywood first became famous not for its movie stars but for its bananas, pineapples, and lemons. Even in winter, tropical fruit thrived under the sunny skies and ocean breezes of the unique temperate zone at the base of the Santa Monica Mountains. Beginning in 1900, tourists came to marvel at Hollywood's gardens and soak up the sun.

In 1907, the warm weather attracted a movie company from back East. Early movie cameras needed plenty of sunlight; during dark, snowy winters it was impossible to film. Hollywood's climate promised year-round filmmaking, and the nearby ocean, mountains, and desert provided scenery that could double for almost anywhere else in the world. Other film companies soon followed, and Hollywood's orchards and fields disappeared as movie sets rose in their place. By 1920, Hollywood studios were producing most of the world's popular films, and stars ranked as its biggest export.

Today movie theaters—palaces as fanciful as the films they showcase—line the streets. Tourists fit their hands and feet into the impressions left by celebrities in the courtyard of Mann's Chinese Theatre. Star shapes bearing famous names decorate the sidewalk. And the stars in the sky shine down on music lovers at the Hollywood Bowl.

Korean Bell of Friendship

ar above the Pacific Ocean, the glorious sound of friendship rings out three times a year from a windy bluff in San Pedro, a fishing and shipping community 20 miles south of downtown Los Angeles. When the 17-ton Korean Bell of Friendship tolls on New Year's Eve, the Fourth of July, and Korean Independence Day (August 15), neighbors in Los Angeles feel the rumble for five minutes after they hear the bell's low, booming tones.

The Republic of Korea gave this ornate bell and pavilion to Los Angeles in 1976 to celebrate the United States bicentennial and to honor the ties between the two countries. Los Angeles is the center of the largest Korean community outside Korea, numbering nearly half a million people.

The bell, which resembles an ancient bronze bell in South Korea, commands a vast view of the Pacific all the way to Santa Catalina Island. Twenty-seven miles across the ocean, wild boar, goats, and bison roam the grassy hills of this wilderness preserve and vacation retreat.

Los Angeles annexed San Pedro in 1906 to gain access to its harbor. Because it was so far away, Los Angeles also added a ribbon of land known as the "Shoestring Strip" to link downtown L.A. to its new port. Today the San Pedro harbor ranks as the busiest on the West Coast.

The Getty Center

High on a hill overlooking Los Angeles, the Getty Center—a college-sized campus dedicated to collecting, preserving, and sharing the world's great art—attracts thousands of visitors to stroll through its gardens, galleries, and plazas. In its libraries and offices, scholars pore over old manuscripts, and conservation scientists develop ways to repair damaged art. The Getty Center, named for the oil tycoon J. Paul Getty, opened in 1997. Getty began collecting art in 1931. When he died in 1976, having built a museum and filled it with America's most impressive collection of Greek and Roman antiquities and French decorative arts, he

bequeathed $750 million of Getty Oil stock to the museum, leading to the creation of the Getty Center.

A tram takes visitors far above the freeway to a plaza surrounded by buildings made of heavy stone blocks imported from Italy. Formed between 8,000 and 80,000 years ago, they contain delicate fossils of feathers, fish, leaves, and shells.

Among the Getty Center's greatest treasures is the view from the top of the hill. The city shimmers below—and on a clear day you can see snowcapped mountains, the glistening Pacific Ocean, and Catalina Island in the distance.

Angels Flight

The shortest railway in the world, Angels Flight™ climbs the steep slope of downtown's Bunker Hill, traveling 350 feet in a little less than a minute. The two angled orange cars with black trim perform a graceful ballet during their short run, gliding over the tracks as one car goes up and the other comes down. A retired Civil War engineer, Colonel J. W. Eddy, opened this tiny railway at the dawn of the twentieth century to link the grand homes atop Bunker Hill with the shops and banks below. Residents rode up and down the hill for a penny instead of huffing and puffing up the steep stairs lining the street. But by 1920, wealthy Angelenos had moved farther west to new, more fashionable neighborhoods, and the Victorian-style mansions on Bunker Hill were divided up into apartments for poorer people hoping for better times and better places ahead.

In the 1960s, the city government decided to remake Bunker Hill. It tore down the once-grand homes, sheared off the top of the steep hill, and erected a forest of glass and granite towers on the newly flat streets. Angels Flight went into storage. Unlike so many other historical aspects of the city, however, it returned, in 1996. Now it ferries people up the hill from Grand Central Market to the office buildings and plazas above. Like a brightly colored time machine, the little railway connects Los Angeles with its past.

Maríachí Plaza

Celebrations call for mariachi music, and it's possible to drive away from Mariachi Plaza in Boyle Heights with an entire fiesta in your car. Mariachi music originated in Mexico. Traditional mariachi bands contain eight or more musicians who play lively, brassy songs. For decades, mariachi musicians have gathered at the corner of First and Boyle, waiting for jobs. Dressed in tight black suits adorned with shiny silver buttons and carrying guitars, accordions, trumpets, and big bass guitars, they're ready to go when drivers pull up to hire them for weddings, birthday parties, or *quinceañeras,* special parties for girls turning 15.

In the 1920s, Boyle Heights served as the center of the Jewish community. But since the 1940s, the East L.A. neighborhood has been home to a primarily Mexican-American population. Colorful murals highlight the area's mariachi traditions. The governor of Jalisco, Mexico, donated the stone *kiosko* in the plaza in 1998, honoring the link between the two countries.

Mariachi Plaza erupts in joyful celebration every November in honor of Saint Cecilia, the patron saint of music, who is especially beloved by the mariachis. Thousands of people enjoy the boisterous bands and spirited dancing that goes on all day in this musical oasis in the midst of the jangling city.

Farmers Market

Shoppers fill their baskets from pyramids of sunny oranges and giant grapefruits at Farmers Market, a fantastic wonderland of little stands selling fresh produce, souvenirs, and various delicacies, located in the Fairfax district. The aromas of freshly baked pies, roasting nuts, and steaming pots of gumbo mingle—and so do tourists and locals alike.

People have loved to gather amid such abundance since the 1930s, when local farmers first trucked their fruits and vegetables to sell at bargain prices in an open field at Third and Fairfax. The idea quickly caught on, and the trucks gave way to permanent wooden stalls, shops, and cafés. At the same time, Jews from the Boyle Heights area in East Los Angeles migrated to the neighborhood, bringing with them the kosher bakeries, delicatessens, and butcher shops that soon lined Fairfax Avenue north of Farmers Market. Over the years, the largely Eastern European Jewish tradition has been enriched by immigrants from the Middle East, Russia, and Ethiopia. On Friday afternoons, when shoppers crowd Fairfax to buy groceries for Sabbath dinner, you can hear a host of languages.

San Fernando Mission

Peacocks roam the manicured lawns of the San Fernando Mission, while water splashes in a flower-shaped fountain. Once a busy ranch and workshop that produced food, wine, blankets, and leather hides for its inhabitants and the brand-new pueblo of Los Angeles, now the church and restored adobe *convento* offer a look into mission life.

San Fernando Rey de España Mission was founded in 1797, the 17th in a chain of 21 missions established by Spanish friars along the coast of California in an effort to convert Native Americans to Catholicism. The priests brought the Indians from their villages to be catechized and baptized and work in the missions' fields and shops. The

missions flourished, but at a high cost. Wrenched from their culture and vulnerable to diseases from the Spaniards, the Native Americans died in large numbers during the more than 70 years of mission rule.

Earthquakes have badly damaged the mission four times since it was built in 1806. The *convento,* with its 4-foot-thick walls and 21 arches, has survived, but the church had to be rebuilt entirely in 1974 after a large quake devastated the San Fernando Valley neighborhood. Nevertheless, it still contains furnishings from the original mission. Babies are baptized within the church's cool darkness, and modern brides and grooms exchange their vows there as they have for centuries.

Beverly Hills

One of the wealthiest communities in the nation arose from a huge lima bean field that grew in the 1880s halfway along the trolley line from downtown Los Angeles to the sea. The trolley stopped at a tiny station in the middle of the field, under a sign that mysteriously proclaimed "Morocco," even though there was nothing there but beans.

Apparently a real estate speculator's dream, Morocco never came to be. In its place, developer Burton E. Green founded Beverly Hills in 1906, an elegantly laid-out town with wide, gently curving streets lined with palm and pepper trees.

In 1919, silent-movie stars from nearby Hollywood began building lavish estates on the lush hillsides of the Santa Monica

Mountains at the north end of Beverly Hills. On the sloping
foothills below, doctors, lawyers, and other well-to-do pro-
fessionals lived in spacious homes. Servants and shopkeepers
occupied neat rows of apartments on the flat streets to
the south.

Between the flats and the foothills lies the Golden
Triangle, a shopping district that includes Rodeo Drive,
known around the world for high-priced luxury. During
the holiday season, Beverly Hills residents march down this
street in a Parade of Lights, which ends with a ceremonial
flip of a switch that bathes the boutiques in sparkling
lights.

Leimert Park Village

The juicy aroma of barbecue and the playful music of steel drums pour into the streets of Leimert Park Village, a neighborhood of small businesses that has emerged as a center of African-American arts and culture. Leimert Park's cafés, galleries, theaters, and nightclubs feature the work of African-American artists. Several times a year, the streets and triangular village green fill with artists and performers celebrating their heritage.

The curving streets were laid out in the 1920s as part of a model community designed by Olmsted and Olmsted, one of the nation's most influential architectural firms. Spanish-style homes nestled in parklike settings, and pedestrian walkways created shortcuts through the blocks.

Like most housing tracts that sprouted all over Los Angeles in the 1920s, Leimert Park prevented people of color from owning homes. But in the 1940s, as many African-Americans came to L.A. to work in wartime industries, the restrictions began to fall. The community spread west from its traditional base along Central Avenue south of downtown. Today a sprawling African-American community finds its heart and its history at Leimert Park Village.

Pasadena

Every New Year's Day, the Tournament of Roses Parade takes over the streets of Pasadena, a city that is Los Angeles' eastern neighbor. Pasadena's settlers first staged the parade in 1890 to celebrate the year-round sunshine and pleasant weather—and to gloat about it in letters and photographs to the folks back home in the Midwest. The balmy weather made Pasadena a resort for rich Midwesterners, who built mansions on "Millionaires' Row" along Orange Grove Avenue. Today hundreds of millions of people gather round their TVs to watch the parade of floral floats and marching bands and the Rose Bowl football game that follows. For many of them, the parade is their most enduring image of sunny Southern California.

Pasadena grew quickly after the region's first freeway opened on New Year's Eve in 1939, linking the city to downtown Los Angeles 10 miles away. It became a center of scientific research, thanks to the Jet Propulsion Library (JPL) and the California Institute of Technology (Caltech). At Caltech in the 1930s, seismologist Charles F. Richter developed a way to measure earthquakes, known today as the Richter scale. The scientists at the world-renowned university still soothe the jittery nerves of Angelenos after every large earthquake with information about how big the shaker was, where it was centered, and along which fault it occurred.

Simon Wiesenthal Center Museum of Tolerance

Dedicated to the memory of Holocaust victims, the Simon Wiesenthal Center Museum of Tolerance challenges visitors with high-tech exhibits and hands-on activities about prejudice, and videos and artifacts of injustices past and present, including the Holocaust. During the museum's construction, the city erupted in racial violence. By the time the museum opened in 1993, it included an interactive survey allowing viewers to express their opinions on racial attitudes in L.A. Today schoolchildren, police officers, teachers, and other groups tour the museum, learning valuable lessons in getting along with others in a city where 100 different languages are spoken and half the residents are from other countries.

More About L.A. People and Places

1542 Explorer Juan Cabrillo sails into San Pedro Bay and notices a layer of smoke from Native American campfires hanging over the land. He names the area "Bay of Smokes." His is the first account of the effects of the "inversion layer," warm air that sits like a lid on top of the Los Angeles basin, preventing pollution from blowing away.

1769 Father Juan Crespi, on the initial Spanish expedition to what will become Los Angeles, writes the first account of an L.A. earthquake, which knocked a soldier off his horse and "lasted as long as half an Ave Maria."

1781 A party of settlers founded a new pueblo named for the Queen of Angels. Today most historians maintain that the original name was "El Pueblo de la Reina de Los Angeles," despite popular use of a mistaken longer version: "El Pueblo de Nuestra Señora la Reina de Los Angeles."

1851 A young African-American slave named Biddy Mason is brought by her owners to Los Angeles, where slavery is illegal. (California entered the Union as a free state in 1850.) She wins freedom for her family in court and, using her wages as a nurse and midwife to acquire property, goes on to become a major downtown landowner. In 1872, she helps organize the First African Methodist Episcopal Church, the oldest African-American church in the city. Today a small park on the Spring Street site of her home honors Biddy Mason's memory.

1884 Writer Charles Lummis walks all the way from Cincinnati, Ohio, to Los Angeles, where he becomes city editor of the *Los Angeles Times* and later the city librarian. His enthusiastic writings lure other artists and writers to Los Angeles. He establishes the California Landmarks Club to preserve L.A.'s historic buildings and helps found the Southwest Museum in Highland Park to study the region's native cultures. He builds a stone house with his own hands, which now serves as headquarters for the Historical Society of Southern California.

1887 Los Angeles finds itself in the midst of a boom. Railroads lower fares to a dollar for a transcontinental trip to L.A. Real-estate developers tout the healthful advantages of Los Angeles' climate.

1892 Edward Doheny strikes oil, launching another major boom in L.A. Drilling rigs sprout up throughout the region, with some areas of the city becoming virtual boomtowns. The substance that trapped Ice Age mammals 40,000 years ago creates fortunes for tycoons and for average people who find themselves lucky enough to live in the middle of an oil field.

1904 Abbot Kinney creates Venice of America. He hopes to make it a center of fine art and music, like Venice, Italy, but finds to his dismay that his customers prefer a carnival with rides and games. Disappointed, he gives them what they want.

1909 L.A.'s first movie studios are built in the Echo Park neighborhood. Soon the Keystone Kops, the Bathing Beauties, and Laurel & Hardy film their antics outside, transforming the community of Echo Park into a huge slapstick movie set.

1913 Engineer William Mulholland opens the Los Angeles Aqueduct, bringing water from the Owens Valley to Los Angeles. As tens of thousands people watch, many of them holding tin cups to grab a taste, Mulholland opens the floodgates, gestures to the roaring water, and says, "There it is. Take it." The new water source allows developers to build housing tracts all across the city, especially in the San Fernando Valley.

1920   The movie industry takes over Hollywood. Dozens of studios operate on Sunset Boulevard near Gower Street. Cowboys line up at the corner, hoping for roles in Westerns, and the area becomes known as Gower Gulch. There's no holly to speak of in Hollywood. The name struck the fancy of Harvey Wilcox's wife after she met a woman on a train who had a summer home named "Hollywood." Wilcox owned the land that became Hollywood.

1921   Simon Rodia begins building Watts Towers. He offers neighborhood children a penny for every piece of broken crockery they bring him, until parents complain that their children are deliberately breaking dishes to earn money.

1923   Aimee Semple McPherson builds a huge circular church across from Echo Park Lake. A beautiful, charismatic minister who feeds the hungry and is said to heal the sick, she is called the most popular woman in Los Angeles. Tour buses bring thousands to hear her; across the country thousands more listen on the radio. In 1926, she disappears in the Santa Monica surf. A month later, 100,000 fans greet her when she returns to L.A. claiming to have been kidnapped. Soon many are disappointed to learn she had actually just run off with her boyfriend.

1924   A film crew brings 14 buffalo to Catalina Island to recreate the American plains for a Western movie. The crew leaves the buffalo behind. Today hundreds of their descendants roam the island's protected wilderness area.

1926   Christine Sterling launches a campaign to preserve Olvera Street, and the Chief of Police allows her to use prison work gangs. "One of the prisoners is a good carpenter, another an electrician. Each night I pray they will arrest a bricklayer and a plumber," she writes in her diary.

1928   Los Angeles' City Hall opens. The tallest building in downtown, its unprecedented 28 stories dwarf everything around it. At the top, a revolving light called the Charles Lindbergh Beacon warns off low-flying planes. Today, dozens of skyscrapers tower over City Hall, the tallest reaching 73 stories.

1932   Los Angeles hosts the Summer Olympics in the Los Angeles Memorial Coliseum, newly enlarged for the occasion to seat 105,000 people. Country Club Drive becomes Olympic Boulevard in time for the event, which brings 400,000 visitors and $50 million to the city.

1933   On March 10, just before 6 P.M., a major earthquake strikes, killing more than 100 people in the heavily populated areas of Long Beach, Garden Grove, Torrance, and Compton, south of L.A. It is the first earthquake for many newcomers—but not the last. The L.A. region experiences dozens of earthquakes a day, most of them too small to feel.

1935   Soon after the Griffith Observatory opens, a monkey escapes from the nearby zoo and climbs onto a model of the moon in the observatory's Hall of Science. It takes three hours, distinguished scientists, and a bunch of bananas to coax the monkey down from its perch and return the moon to its orbit. Afterward, the observatory's director says, "Don't tell me now there's not life on the moon."

1938   Christine Sterling masterminds "China City," a tourist attraction offering a romanticized image of a street in China. Featuring movie sets and actors hired to portray "typical" Chinese, it soon burns down. No one tries to rebuild it.

1939   Nathanael West's *The Day of the Locust* and Raymond Chandler's *The Big Sleep* are published. Depicting a grim, desperate underside to L.A.'s sunny surface, the novels are considered definitive, continuing to influence perceptions to this day.

1942   After Japan bombs Pearl Harbor at the start of World War II, Japanese-American residents of Little Tokyo are rounded up and transported to detention camps hundreds of miles away. African-

Americans, coming to Los Angeles in increasing numbers for wartime jobs, move into the abandoned community, one of the few neighborhoods where they can find housing. Little Tokyo fosters a lively nightlife, with clubs featuring some of the biggest musicians of the Big Band era.

1951   "This is the city," intones Jack Webb at the beginning of every episode of "Dragnet," a popular TV show based on actual cases from the Los Angeles Police Department. Airing until 1959, "Dragnet" returns eight years later for a three-year run in color.

1958   The Brooklyn Dodgers relocate to Los Angeles, bringing with them announcer Vin Scully, whose voice becomes the soundtrack to summer afternoons for generations of Angelenos. He begins each game with "A very pleasant good afternoon to you, wherever you may be...."

1961   The last Red Car stops running, ending an era. The Red Car trolleys had traveled on tracks throughout the L.A. area since the turn of the century, at a cost of about a penny a mile. Increasing traffic and the efforts of auto, tire, and petroleum companies usher in the age of the freeway.

1962   Dodger Stadium opens in Chavez Ravine, on April 10, with a team that includes future baseball legends Sandy Koufax, Don Drysdale, and Maury Wills. In 1963, they win the World Series.

1965   The South-Central community of Watts erupts in violence and looting after police officers try to arrest a young African-American motorist for drunk driving. The violence calls attention to the poverty in South-Central.

1973   Tom Bradley becomes L.A.'s first African-American mayor. He will lead the city for the next 20 years. During his five terms in office, the city will develop a major skyline and emerge as the leading trading partner with the Pacific Rim.

1984   Los Angeles becomes the first American city to host two Olympics. The 1984 Summer Olympic Games are considered by many to be Mayor Bradley's finest hour, as L.A. stages a profitable, peaceful, well-organized event. In fact, because of efforts to organize carpools and flexible work hours, traffic flows better during the Olympics than ever before— or since.

1992   Violence, looting, and arson erupt in Los Angeles when four police officers are found not guilty of beating Rodney King, an African-American man stopped for speeding. After days of unrest, King appears on television to tearfully ask, "Can we all get along?" The nearly weeklong civil strife leaves burned-out buildings throughout the city and creates a massive effort to bring economic development to the inner city.

1994   On January 17 at 4:31 A.M., the Northridge earthquake strikes with a magnitude of 6.8, killing more than 60 people, injuring more than 6,000 others, and destroying or seriously damaging more than 1,000 buildings. Freeway overpasses collapse and more than 20,000 people lose their homes. It is one of the costliest disasters in American history.

1998   Workers next to Watts Towers uncover the buried remains of a red 1927 Hudson automobile, solving an old mystery. In the late 1920s and early 1930s, Simon Rodia, the towers' creator, was rumored to drive a red Hudson equipped with a fire engine siren. Whenever he got to a red light, he would crank up the siren and speed through the intersection. The police issued a warrant for the driver of the car, but the car was never found, and Rodia was never proved to be the culprit. Apparently, he buried the evidence next to his towers.

About the Authors

JULIE JASKOL and BRIAN LEWIS met in 1987 when they were both reporters for the Los Angeles Independent Newspapers, a group of weekly newspapers that has been covering Los Angeles neighborhoods for seventy-five years. As reporters, they combed their community for news and features that captured the elusive "essence" of Los Angeles. They contacted local elected officials, activists, artists, merchants, teachers, parents, and children all involved in the public life of their city. Later, Ms. Jaskol took a job as press deputy to Los Angeles City Councilmember Michael Woo. In that capacity, she worked in historic City Hall during some of Los Angeles's most tumultuous recent history: the Rodney King trial and the civil unrest. Her work in City Hall took her from Baptist churches in South-Central to crumbling tenements in Pico-Union, from the gated homes of celebrities in Bel-Air to the predawn produce market downtown. Today she is Director of Communications and Public Affairs for The Los Angeles Free Clinic, a 32-year-old nonprofit institution that plays a leading role in improving the lives of Los Angeles's homeless and working poor.

Brian Lewis, an award-winning journalist and columnist, has risen to Editor of the Los Angeles Independent Newspapers, overseeing coverage of communities from downtown to the Westside. In working on this book, Ms. Jaskol and Mr. Lewis called on preservationists, artists, community leaders, and local activists to help create an image of Los Angeles enriched by the intimate knowledge and great love these people have for their hometown. They took walking tours, visited festivals, and picked through handwritten histories in cramped libraries. (For many communities, published histories simply don't exist.) And they ate good food!

As other friends and even family have left the city for quieter, cheaper, "safer" places in which to raise their children, Julie and Brian prefer Los Angeles's depth, challenge, and variety—not to mention the weather. They are proud that their two children are third-generation Angelenos, raised with the richness L.A. has to offer.

About the Illustrator

ELISA KLEVEN, a native of Los Angeles, says, "When I was five, my mother took me to visit Watts Towers. The magical spires, assembled from plaster and seashells, tiles and glass, inspired me to make my own miniature towers of clay, beads, and bottle caps. And, who knows, maybe my grown-up urge to create the little collage worlds inside my picture books also has something to do with that long-ago visit to Watts." Ms. Kleven says that in the process of illustrating this book she enjoyed discovering new parts of her home city and revisiting places she'd loved as a child. She maintains close ties to Los Angeles through her family and friends, among them Julie Jaskol whom she's known since they were freshmen together at U.C. Berkeley.

Ms. Kleven is an award-winning author and illustrator whose work is beloved by children, parents, teachers, and booksellers alike. Her many outstanding picture books include *Abuela,* by Arthur Dorros; *De Colores* and *Diez Deditos,* both by José-Luis Orozco; and her own *The Paper Princess, The Puddle Pail, A Monster in the House,* and *Hooray, a Piñata!* Elisa Kleven lives in Albany, California, with her husband, Paul; her daughter, Mia; her son, Ben; and their dog and cat.

COVER ART   *The largest lotus bed outside China blooms in Echo Park Lake, shown in the lower right corner of the jacket. Every July the lotuses form the backdrop to the Lotus Festival, celebrating Asian and Pacific Island culture. Los Angeles' first suburban neighborhood of homes took root along Echo Park Lake. When downtown got too crowded in the 1880s, people created a more peaceful residential community in Echo Park, building Victorian homes that have been preserved in all their gingerbread glory on Carroll Avenue. Generation after generation has sought the perfect suburb by creating new neighborhoods and cities over all the available land from the mountains on the north, south, and east to the ocean on the west. Dodger Stadium crowned a hill in Echo Park in 1962, and most of the downtown skyline and the freeways that ring it rose in the 1960s and 1970s, when redevelopment gave the area a facelift.*

TITLE PAGE ART   *When the Los Angeles Central Library opened in 1927, its architect boasted that the building could withstand both earthquakes and fires. Unfortunately, the books couldn't. In 1986 two fires destroyed 800,000 books and damaged 800,000 others. A massive volunteer effort saved nearly all of the damaged books by painstakingly freezing and then treating each volume rescued from the blaze. The building, which was virtually undamaged, reopened in 1993 with a new wing. With more than two million books, the L.A. Central Library is the largest research library west of the Mississippi. A welcoming inscription over the entrance proclaims, "Books invite all, they constrain none."*